Bored No More!

Quiz Book

by Aubre Andrus

★ American Girl®

Published by American Girl Publishing

16 17 18 19 20 21 22 LEO 11 10 9 8 7 6 5 4 3 2

Editorial Development: Carrie Anton
Art Direction & Design: Camela Decaire
Production: Judith Lary, Sarah Boecher, Jeannette Bailey, Tami Kepler

Illustrations: Carol Yoshizumi

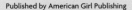

americangirl.com/service

Dear Reader,

The quizzes in this book will help you get through the dull days that bring on the snores. Start by selecting a quiz and answering the questions. Add up the answers to see what your responses say about you. But unlike other quiz books, the fun doesn't stop there!

Each quiz leads to three or more activities that will brighten up your boring day because they're based specifically on how you answered the quiz questions. If there's a tie between two answers, read them both; then choose the one that appeals to you right now.

Remember that you can take each quiz more than once because your moods and interests may change. There are all kinds of activities at the end of each quiz that you can do on your own or with a group, so you don't want to miss out!

Or skip the quizzes and choose any activity that catches your eye. You'll find a bunch of extra ideas at the end of some quizzes along with a big list of boredom busters on page 78.

Skip the snores, beat the bores, and find the fun!

Your friends at American Girl

Safety Note
Any time you see this hand or when you think a project or recipe is too hard to do yourself, ask an adult to help you. Be sure an adult supervises any cutting or cooking. Also make sure you keep small pieces, such as beads and rhinestones, put away so that younger siblings don't eat them!

Table of Contents

Fun with One

Turn your solo time into so-fun time!

1. When I'm busy, I wish I could spend more time
 a. hanging out at home.
 b. reading or watching a movie.
 c. cuddling with my pet.

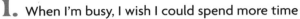

2. My dream vacation is
 a. swimming off the beaches of a tropical island.
 b. an adventure trip in the jungle.
 c. horseback riding in the Grand Canyon.

3. Sometimes I feel as though I don't take enough time to
 a. relax.
 b. get good at a hobby.
 c. help out with chores.

4. I would love to work at a
 a. swimming pool.
 b. library.
 c. shelter for animals.

5. My dream bedroom
 a. has a beautiful view of mountains.
 b. is a tree house.
 c. has a special bed for my pet, too.

6. Sometimes I think I
  a. want to try yoga.
  b. will be famous someday.
  c. can read my pet's thoughts.

7. When my bedroom is messy, you'll find
  a. my dresser overrun with hair accessories.
  b. art supplies everywhere.
  c. my pet's toys lying around.

8. The perfect gift for me is a
  a. yummy-smelling bottle of lotion.
  b. brand-new book.
  c. cuddly stuffed animal.

9. If I worked on a movie set, I'd be the
  a. hair or makeup artist.
  b. writer or art director.
  c. animal trainer for the furry stars.

Answers

Special Spa

If you picked **more a's,** have a relaxing spa day at home. Turn on some calming music, and sip a glass of cool water with a cucumber slice floating on top. Here are a few spa activities to try:

- Apply a store-bought face mask, and then place cucumber slices on your eyes while you lie down to let the mask dry.

- Spritz your hair with water and comb through. Now spritz some leave-in conditioner onto your damp hair. Let your hair air-dry for a nice natural style.

- In a small bowl, mix equal parts sugar and baby oil. Scrub your hands with the mixture, and then rinse with warm water. Dry hands, and finish with soothing hand lotion.

Extreme Dreams

If you picked **more b's,** you dream big and can often be found imagining creative things. Why not create a dream journal to keep all of your hopes and wishes? Decorate the cover of a regular note-book with colored paper and stickers. Divide your journal into chapters, such as "Dream Vacations," "Dream Jobs," and "My Favorite Dreams." Capture your real dreams, your daydreams, and any other wishes and hopes you have.

Pet Playdate

If you picked **more c's,** have a Pet Pal Day. Spend an afternoon playing with your favorite furry friend. Does your dog love going for long walks? Does your cat prefer to cuddle on your bed? Give your pet extra-special attention that you might not have time to give on a busier day. It's a perfect chance to take cute pictures of the two of you or draw some portraits of your happy pet. Who doesn't love to feel loved?

Art Starts

Try some creative ways to drive away dull days!

1. I feel most inspired when I
   a. visit a new place.
   b. see beautiful photos or drawings.
   c. make something with my hands.

2. When I have a group project at school, I like to
   a. design an informational poster.
   b. write a story, create a costume, and act it out.
   c. create a 3D diorama or display.

3. I carry my books in a
   a. messenger bag decorated with flowers I drew using fabric markers.
   b. backpack with a bold, colorful print.
   c. tote bag I made myself.

4. I could see myself becoming a(n)
   a. art teacher.
   b. graphic designer.
   c. store owner.

5. In my desk drawer, you'll find
   a. colored pencils.
   b. stickers and rhinestones.
   c. beads of every size and shape.

6. My assignment notebook is filled with
   a. doodles every day of the week.
   b. notes about all kinds of activities, such as music lessons, soccer practice, and volunteer opportunities.
   c. pictures of my friends and family.

7. When planning a party, I can't wait to
   a. hang decorations.
   b. pick the theme.
   c. bake cupcakes.

Answers

Mixed Media

If you chose **more a's,** pick up a paintbrush and make a scene! You love to doodle, but instead of a pencil, try using watercolor paints. Create an imaginary wonderland, make a memory from your last vacation, or mirror the view from your bedroom window. Let the painting dry, and then finish your masterpiece with colored pencil outlines and other drawn details.

Inspiration Board

If you chose **more c's,** channel your creative energy into a project that will inspire you every hour of every day! Pictures spark your imagination, so find interesting images in magazines or newspapers or from your own travels. Glue them to a poster board along with scraps of pretty colored paper, patterned fabric, and anything else that makes you smile. Hang the poster above your desk. Whenever you're feeling down or you're stuck on a homework assignment, look to your poster to brighten your mood and inspire your mind!

Recycled Style

If you chose **more b's,** turn old T-shirts into pretty accessories. Ask a parent if it's OK to cut one or two colorful T-shirts into long, thin strips. Have someone hold the ends of three strips while you braid them together. Then turn the braids into one of these accessories:

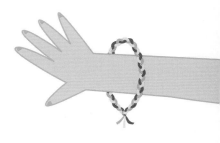

Headband
Size the braid around your head and tie it into a tight knot at the nape of your neck. Remove the band from your head, and trim the ends.

Bracelet
Ask an adult to knot the braid loosely around your wrist so that you can slide it off easily. Trim the ends.

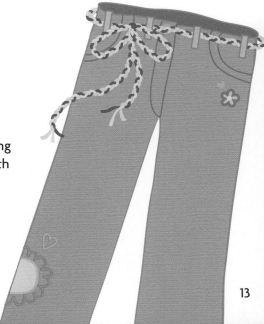

Belt
Slip the braid through your belt loops. Make sure it's long enough with plenty of length left over. Double-knot the ends. When you wear the belt, tie it into a loose bow at your side.

Rainy-Day Fun

Stuck inside on a rainy day? Find the perfect trick to chase away the gloom.

1. Lately, I haven't had any time to
   a. be creative.
   b. learn something new.
   c. go to the library.

2. When it comes to books, I love to
   a. write them myself.
   b. read a chapter out loud.
   c. read them alone, silently.

3. On my shelves, you will find
   a. handmade projects from art class.
   b. trophies and awards.
   c. my favorite novels.

4. When I'm really busy with boring things like chores, I look forward to a free moment so that I can
   a. finish that craft project I started last week.
   b. think about what new class or sport I'm going to sign up for next.
   c. flip through the pages of a magazine.

5. For Halloween, I like to dress in
   a. creative costumes that I made myself.
   b. make-believe costumes such as a fairy or pirate.
   c. classic costumes such as a black cat or creepy witch.

6. In the winter, I like to
   a. bake my favorite holiday cookies with my grandma.
   b. get in the holiday spirit by decorating my home.
   c. curl up with a warm blanket and watch a holiday movie.

7. My favorite kind of activity books are the kinds with
   a. cool crafts for me to make.
   b. quizzes that teach me all about what my personality means.
   c. puzzles and trivia that boggle my mind.

Answers

Rainbow Ribbon Curtain

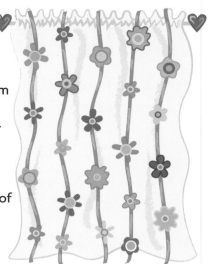

If you picked **more a's,** brighten the view from your window with a curtain of rainbow ribbons. Attach felt flowers randomly along lengths of ribbon with Glue Dots®. Make your own felt flowers by cutting a flower-petal shape from felt and attaching a button center with a Glue Dot. Ask a parent to help you attach the ribbons to the top of your curtains with safety pins.

Fantasy Storyteller

If you picked **more b's,** turn old mismatched playing cards (you need only about 25 cards) into a clever—and silly—deck of fortune-telling tools by covering the number side of the cards with paper. To do this, outline the card on a piece of colored paper, cut out the shape, and glue it to the card. Doodle simple drawings of a person or place, or write a word or number on each card.

Here are some examples:

- the number 7
- a picture of snow falling
- the word "funny"
- a picture of a dog
- a picture of three horses

To tell someone's fortune, shuffle the cards facedown and ask your friend to draw 6 cards. Now ask her to give 3 of those cards back to you without looking at them. Now add 2 cards of your own choice. Flip over all 5 cards. Create a detailed story that uses all 5 cards and begins with, "In the future. . ."

For example, "In the future. . . you will adopt a golden retriever on a snowy day in December. You'll find the dog at a farm with beautiful horses galloping out back and a funny mailbox in the front yard. You'll give the dog a name with 7 letters in it."

Solo Book Club

If you picked **more c's,** start your own personal book club! Make a list of all the books you want to read, and write them down on a long construction-paper rectangle—this will be your bookmark. Now create a comfy reading spot in your room. It could be a chair, a corner with pillows and blankets, or a big pillow propped up right on your bed. Make sure your spot has good light.

Set a goal, such as reading one book per week or month. Schedule time after school or on the weekends for your special reading time. When you finish a book, place a star sticker on your bookmark.

Perfect Party

The decorations are set, but you still need to entertain your guests! Take this quiz to find out which activity is just right for your celebration.

1. The guests have arrived! It's
   a. everyone from class.
   b. a few girls from school and a few more from my Girl Scout troop.
   c. my two best friends.

2. At my party, everyone
   a. knows one another.
   b. knows me, but they don't all know each other.
   c. is best friends with each other.

3. At my dream party, I would
   a. see a Broadway musical.
   b. design my own real ball gown.
   c. taste-test every ice cream flavor in the world.

4. Everyone here likes to
   a. make up dances.
   b. make crafts.
   c. eat sweets.

5. My dream present is a
  a. karaoke machine.
  b. sewing machine.
  c. snow-cone maker.

6. In my free time, I like to
  a. listen to music.
  b. doodle and draw.
  c. try a new recipe.

7. I'm not afraid to
  a. perform in front of people.
  b. show off my artistic skills.
  c. try new foods.

8. My friends always
  a. laugh at my jokes.
  b. ask me how I made that.
  c. like to eat at my house.

9. At sleepovers, my friends and I usually
  a. act out silly skits.
  b. do each other's hair.
  c. create crazy ice cream
       sundaes.

19

Answers

Dance-a-thon

If you chose **more a's,** your friends love to have fun together and are anything but shy. Your party's the perfect chance for them to dance the night away and sing along to their favorite songs! Before the party, create a playlist of dance music and ask a parent to clear some space for a dance party. Set out a box of fun props, such as feather boas, sunglasses, and hats. Ask a parent to hang holiday lights around the dance floor. Add a few balloons just for fun.

When your guests all arrive, dim the lights and start dancing! Take turns teaching each other new moves. As a group, make up a special dance and give it a name. Ask an adult or sibling to take some pictures and video of your entire group performing your newly created move.

Bitty Jewelry Box

If you chose **more b's,** have your guests turn mint tins into palm-sized cases for their accessories. They can personalize the outside of their box by gluing a pretty patterned paper to the top and attaching adhesive rhinestones in the shape of their first initial. On the inside, they can glue a piece of felt to the bottom and attach a tiny mirror (get these at a craft store) to the lid with Glue Dots. This bitty box is perfect for packing in a suitcase or a backpack.

Extra Sweet Pizza Treat

If you chose **more c's,** make your own dessert after dinner—an extra sweet pizza treat! Ask a parent to bake sugar cookie dough into one giant round cookie. After the cookie has cooled, gather your guests and start to create your sweet pizza masterpiece. Cover the cookie with frosting and then top with soft candy, fruit slices, and sprinkles. Ask an adult to slice the cookie like a pizza. Enjoy!

**Here are a few more activities
you and your guests will love:**

• If not all guests know each other, start off by playing an icebreaker, such as Two Truths and a Lie. Guests take turns telling everyone three things—two things that are true and one that is made up. It's up to the rest of the group to guess which one is the lie.

• Hold a screening of a newly released movie, complete with low lights, popcorn, and candy.

• Have a video game competition with your favorite dance or karaoke video game.

• Pick a buzzword for your guests to avoid, such as "dance," "present," or "cake." Any guest caught saying the buzzword has to wear a gift bow on her head!

• Hide the party favor bags around the party area. Then give your guests a few clues for a scavenger hunt.

• Ask a sibling or family member to play DJ and keep good tunes playing all party long for your guests.

• Stage a silly group photo complete with funny props, hats, and sunglasses.

• Give guests little handmade crafts for winning any games they played at your party.

Sibling Harmony

Don't fight—fun is in sight! Take this quiz to decide what you and one of your brothers or sisters should do right now.

1. My sibling is
   a. older than I am.
   b. younger than I am.
   c. about the same age.

2. The thing we have in common is that we are both
   a. creative.
   b. involved in a lot of different activities.
   c. hard workers.

3. Our favorite thing to do together on family vacations is
   a. collect seashells and pretty sea glass.
   b. make new friends with kids at the pool.
   c. explore the hotel together.

4. In our rooms, you'll find the same
   a. marker set.
   b. sneakers.
   c. books.

5. When we watch TV together, we watch
   a. cooking shows.
   b. funny shows about people our age.
   c. animal and science shows.

6. Someday, we'll
   a. create an invention to make it easier for siblings to share rooms.
   b. be on the same sports team.
   c. open a restaurant together.

7. Sometimes I wish we could
   a. spend more time goofing off together.
   b. get to know each other better.
   c. do something cool for our parents together.

23

Answers

Game Time

If you picked **more a's,** make a family game. Start with a simple concept. For example, draw a sidewalk-like path with twists and turns on a poster board. Fill in every third square with an action, such as "Move ahead 3 spaces," or "Lose a turn," or "Go back 2 spaces." Around the board, doodle fun landmarks that your sibling and family love to visit.

Next, create cards from different-colored construction paper. Write trivia questions about your family on the cards. Color in the remaining spaces on the board using the same colors as your construction paper cards.

To play the game, roll a pair of dice, and move ahead the number rolled. If you land on a blank square, choose a card; then ask your brother or sister to read the question to you. If you answer correctly, you get to roll again. If you get it wrong, you lose a turn and your sibling gets to roll.

Sibling School

If you picked **more b's,** you and your talented sibling both have at least one special hobby or skill that makes your sibling envious. Why not teach each other something new? Maybe it's a cool doodle, a card trick, or a perfect soccer kick. Or maybe it's a favorite recipe, a hairstyle, or the best way to make a friendship bracelet. Be patient when teaching your sibling—and when it's your turn to learn something new.

Family Feast

If you picked **more c's,** band together to cook up and serve something your parents will love. Whether it's breakfast, lunch, or dessert, food made with love is a great gift—even if you have to ask for help. Here are some ideas:

- **Breakfast:** Spread peanut butter onto a wrap and then roll it around a banana. Serve with a glass of milk and a side of strawberries.

- **Lunch:** Make sandwiches with ham, cheddar cheese, and lettuce. Serve with a side of grapes and a glass of juice.

- **Dessert:** Create a signature sundae that represents everything your parents love. Use different flavors of ice cream and toppings for a one-of-a-kind combination. Then give it a special name.

Kitchen Conundrum

Want to bake or make something special but don't know where to start? Answer this quick questionnaire to help point you toward a simple snack that's fun to create—and delicious to eat.

1. After school, I like to
   a. grab a chewy granola bar to go.
   b. pour a glass of cold juice.
   c. sit down for a filling mini meal.

4. I can't get enough
   a. chocolate.
   b. fruit.
   c. cheese.

2. I like to
   a. follow recipes exactly.
   b. create my own recipes from scratch.
   c. add a dash of this and that to make a recipe fun and exciting.

3. When I cook, I prefer to use the
   a. oven (with help from a parent) to bake something delicious.
   b. freezer to make a frozen treat.
   c. counter and a few utensils for a quick bite to eat.

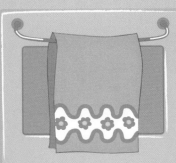

5. My favorite part about cooking is
  a. the yummy smells that fill the kitchen.
  b. creating new flavors.
  c. eating!

6. I plan to share my delicious dish with
  a. my friends.
  b. my family.
  c. myself. . . and maybe one other person.

7. My favorite thing to eat is something
  a. super sweet like candy.
  b. chilled and refreshing on a warm day.
  c. savory like cheese and crackers.

Answers

Cupcake Cookies

If you answered **more a's,** treat yourself to cookies made from packaged cake mix. To make the batter, just follow the directions on the box. But instead of pouring the batter into a cupcake tin, scoop 1-inch balls of batter onto a greased cookie sheet. Bake at the temperature listed on the box for 10–15 minutes or until the edges are golden brown. Once the cookies have cooled, top with frosting and sprinkles for a new twist on a cupcake taste.

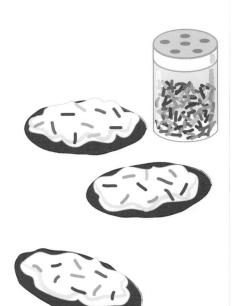

Sweet Sippers

If you answered **more b's,** make a beverage that's delightful to drink by freezing some easy-to-make twice-as-nice ice cubes. Fill ice cube trays with fruit slices and sugar sprinkles or jimmies. Top off each cube with ginger ale, fruit juice, or water. Freeze for a few hours, and then add the cubes to your drink for a refreshing twist. Try these combinations:

- strawberry slices + ginger ale ice cubes dropped into apple juice
- sugar sprinkles + water ice cubes dropped into ginger ale
- cherries + cherry soda ice cubes dropped into soda

Sandwich Stackers

If you answered **more c's,** turn a simple sandwich into a high-rise fun-to-eat treat. Use a cookie cutter to cut bread into small circles, squares, or silly shapes. Now build your sandwich with your favorite fillings. Stack the sandwich so it's at least three layers tall. Give these combinations a try:

- peanut butter and banana slices on wheat bread

- turkey, ham, cheese, and mayonnaise on potato bread

- cream cheese and crushed potato chips on white bread

cream cheese

29

Doodle on the Double

Is a blank piece of paper tempting you? This quiz will inspire you to do a doodle on the double—but with a twist!

1. When it comes to art, I love using
   a. acrylic paints.
   b. colored pencils.
   c. markers.

2. There's nothing more exciting than visiting
   a. a faraway place.
   b. my friends after school.
   c. wild animals at the zoo.

3. In my bedroom, I have a
   a. beautiful ocean sunset poster.
   b. fun photo collage of all my friends.
   c. super-cute puppy poster.

4. Nothing makes me smile more than pictures of
a. pretty tropical flowers from my vacation.
b. my family acting silly.
c. my cute cat as she sleeps peacefully.

5. I would love to live
a. on top of a magnificent mountain.
b. near a lively park in a city.
c. on a quiet horse ranch.

6. My bedroom has a
a. rainforest theme so that I can pretend I live outdoors.
b. "me" theme. It's a combination of all the stuff I love!
c. cheetah-print theme because animals are my life!

7. My favorite part of scrapbooking is
a. arranging everything on the page.
b. choosing the photos.
c. finding pretty paper and decorations.

Answers

Paper Pieces

If you picked **more a's,** doodle a basic scene such as a sunset, mountain range, or a beautiful flower. Gather paper and tissue paper in different shades of the colors that go best with your picture. Now rip the paper into small pieces. Use a glue stick to attach the pieces to your drawing by overlapping and clustering them until you form a colorful collage of shapes and shades. Let dry.

Pretend Portrait

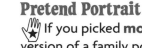 If you picked **more b's,** doodle a silly version of a family portrait. Start by asking an adult for an extra family photo that you can cut up, or make a color photocopy of a family photo. Carefully cut each person's face from the picture. Then use a glue stick to attach the faces to a piece of paper. Now sketch an imaginary scene around the faces. Don't forget the clothes and accessories! Color in the final sketch with markers.

Pet Vignette

If you picked **more c's,** craft a doodle-style pet portrait. Get inspired by your own pets or by your favorite animal. Cut the basic animal shapes from different kinds of patterned and solid scrapbook paper. Cut a body, face, ears, eyes, nose, and mouth. Glue the shapes together and let dry. Add sequins, rhinestones, or paper trimming to finish.

Here are a few more doodles you can do:

• Turn your name into a doodle. Write all the letters. Then turn each one into something you love—an animal, a sport, a place, or an object.

• Print a black-and-white copy of a family photo, and use colored pencils to turn the pic into an explosion of crazy colors.

• Create a logo for yourself. It could be the first letter of your name, the shape of something you love, or a combination of the two. Be sure to use your feel-good colors.

• Design a new cursive signature for yourself. Pretend you're a movie star and create an impressive autograph for your fans!

• Turn your friends into superheroes. Doodle cool costumes and special powers for the cover of a pretend comic book.

• What would you look like if you were an animal? Draw an animal version of yourself by choosing a creature you identify with. Add a few details that are special to you, such as freckles, glasses, or jewelry.

• Re-create a family photo. Don't trace, but use your best sketching skills to create your own special portrait.

After-School De-Stress

It's been a long, hard day at school, and you need to do something fun and relaxing. But what will clear your mind and calm you down? Take this quiz for creative ideas on how to chill out.

1. Overall, today was a
- **a.** busy day.
- **b.** difficult day.
- **c.** disappointing day.

2. At school today, I
- **a.** had a pop quiz in the morning, threw a surprise celebration at lunch for my friend's birthday, and volunteered to help a younger student with her math flash cards.
- **b.** took a science test for which I studied all week.
- **c.** had a fight with a close friend.

3. If I had a full day to do whatever I wanted, I would
- **a.** take a bike ride on my favorite bike path.
- **b.** doodle my heart out with a fresh box of colored pencils.
- **c.** spend every second of it with my best friend.

4. My dream vacation is
- **a.** a trip to the amusement park with all my friends.
- **b.** a week on a tropical beach with my best friend.
- **c.** a long summer weekend at a cabin with my entire family.

5. To calm my nerves, I
- **a.** tap my fingers or fidget.
- **b.** breathe slowly and close my eyes.
- **c.** talk it out with someone who understands.

6. I don't like to
- **a.** be alone.
- **b.** speak in front of a lot of people.
- **c.** keep my feelings to myself.

7. I spend my free time
- **a.** playing sports.
- **b.** making crafts.
- **c.** babysitting.

8. Right now, I'm in a ____ mood.
- **a.** hyper
- **b.** stressed-out
- **c.** sad

9. When it comes to my group of friends, I'm the
- **a.** center of attention.
- **b.** math whiz.
- **c.** shy one.

Answers

Sibling School

If you picked **more a's,** today was a busy day and you're a little wound up. Use your energy to help a sibling. Teach your sibling something new, whether it's how to doodle a dog, shoot a layup, or play the piano. There's definitely something you know how to do that your brother or sister would love to learn. Don't have any siblings? Teach a parent or friend!

Time Out

If you picked **more b's,** today was a little stressful. Take 30 minutes to yourself to calm down. Relax on your bed or in a quiet place with a good book. Even if you get through only a few pages, an engaging story will surely put a smile on your face. And smiling is a great way to beat stress.

Mom and Me Meal

If you picked **more c's,** you might be feeling a little blue today. Help your mom make dinner. You'll learn something new and get some alone time to talk about your day. Clear your mind by telling her anything that's bothering you. Ask her for advice, and then focus on helping your mom. Remember, tomorrow's a new day!

Road-Trip Remedy

Stuck in a car that seems to be creeping along? Find the perfect activity for a long drive home or away.

1. What other passengers are in the car with you, besides the driver?
   a. just me
   b. my siblings
   c. my entire family

2. We're driving
   a. for less than an hour.
   b. for a few hours.
   c. for what seems like forever!

3. When I look out the window, I see
   a. neighborhoods.
   b. long stretches of highway.
   c. a new city in a new state.

4. My favorite kind of game is
   a. active games like charades.
   b. classic card games.
   c. seek-and-find picture games.

5 miles

5. When it comes to winning, I
  a. would rather play a game in which we all work together.
  b. like using a strategy to slowly take the win.
  c. love to race and see who wins.

6. If I have no plans at home, the first thing I do is
  a. talk to my friends.
  b. start an art project.
  c. watch a movie.

7. When traveling, I prefer to have a
  a. friend or sibling to keep me entertained.
  b. pencil and a notepad.
  c. magazine.

Answers

Quizzing Questions

If you chose **more a's,** take turns asking a question. It could be a "would you rather. . ." question or a "what's your favorite. . ." question, or anything else that pops into your mind. The catch is that the adults have to answer the question as if they are 10 years old. And you have to answer the question as if you are an adult. You'll have to take a guess at what you think you'll be like, and you'll learn what your parent was like as a kid. Here are some questions to get you started:

- Would you rather read the book or see the movie?
- What's your favorite item of clothing?
- Would you rather go camping or go to a resort?
- What's your favorite class in school?
- Would you rather live in a mansion or a tree house?
- What's your favorite meal of the day?
- Would you rather play or watch a sport?
- What's your favorite dessert in the whole world?
- Would you rather go snorkeling in the ocean or snowboarding down a mountain?
- What's your dream job?

Wordy Way

If you chose **more b's,** here are a few classic word games that will keep you busy:

- **Spell It Out:** The goal of the game is to spell a word one letter at a time to make the word as long as possible. The first person gets to pick the first letter. By going back and forth, players try to make the word as long as they can. The player who completes the word is awarded a point for each letter in the word. If a player gets stuck and can't add a letter, she loses 1 point.

- **Categories:** One person thinks of a category in her head and then starts naming out loud things that fit within the category. The other players have to guess what the category is. Set a time limit (such as 1 minute) or a distance limit (such as 1 mile). Award 1 point every time a player guesses the correct category.

- **Winning Words:** Pick a letter. Players have 1 minute to write down as many words as they can that begin with that letter. When the minute is up, players read their lists aloud. Players get 1 point for each word that no one else thought of. Take turns picking the letter.

Go-Go Bingo

If you chose **more c's,** then bingo is your game-o. A bingo game can last for hours, so it's the perfect game to keep an entire vehicle of passengers entertained on a long road trip. Brainstorm together to create a giant checklist of items for which the entire family can be on the lookout. When anyone finds one of the items, write that person's initials next to the item. The first to 10 wins!

Here's a list to get you started:

- a fast-food restaurant at which you've never eaten
- a city you've never visited before
- a yellow sports car
- a red shirt
- a green house
- a dog in another car
- someone eating ice cream in a car
- a Wisconsin license plate
- a kayak on top of a car
- two bikes on top of a car
- a blue van

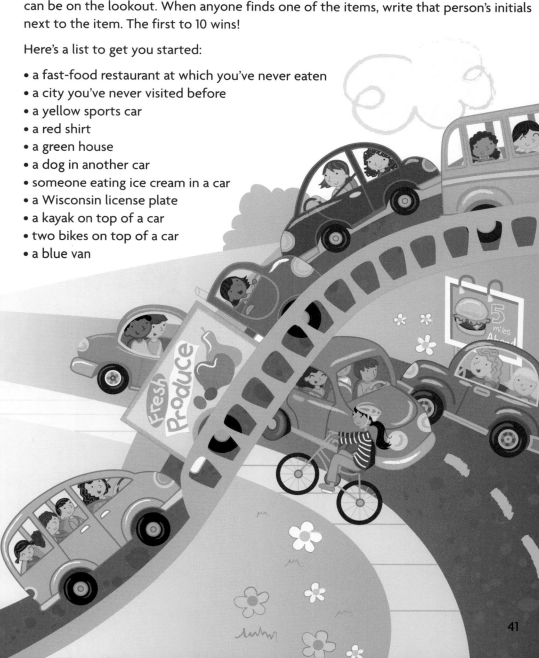

Fun with Friends

Hanging out with your pals but can't decide what to do?
Take this quiz together to find a great idea for the group.

1. Today, we want to
   a. stay inside.
   b. get outdoors because the weather is perfect.
   c. do something active, no matter where it is.

2. My friends and I
   a. act silly all the time.
   b. like to help others.
   c. are outgoing.

3. Our teachers would call us a
   a. creative bunch.
   b. friendly group.
   c. sporty squad.

4. Our most fun day together was when we
   a. put on a play for our parents.
   b. volunteered at the animal shelter.
   c. rode bikes around town.

5. If we were animals, we would be
   a. monkeys.
   b. dogs.
   c. cheetahs.

6. The name of our made-up theme song would be
   a. "Take the Stage."
   b. "Show Some Love, Give a Hug."
   c. "Sporty Sisters Win Again."

7. Someday, you'll find us
   a. winning Academy Awards.
   b. running a charity for kids.
   c. playing in a national championship sports game.

8. All together, we have a lot of
   a. craft supplies.
   b. other friends.
   c. sports equipment.

9. When we watch a movie together, it's always a
   a. silly comedy.
   b. sweet but sad drama.
   c. fun action movie.

Answers

Friendly Film

If you chose **more a's,** use your bright personalities and creativity to make a movie. Ask a parent or sibling to film you. When you're done, premiere the movie to your family and friends—complete with popcorn!

Here are some ideas to get you started:

- a musical, complete with singing and costume changes

- a comedy skit with short scenes that will make your friends and neighbors giggle

- a mystery movie in which something important goes missing and the only way to resolve the situation is by following the clues

Helping Hearts

If you chose **more b's,** you and your friends have kind hearts and good spirits. Today's a great day to get outside and make a difference.

Here are some ideas to get you started:

- With an adult as your guide, head to a public space such as a playground or park and clean up garbage there. Make sure to bring garbage bags and plastic gloves, and beware of broken glass.

- Ask an elderly neighbor you know if she needs help raking leaves, shoveling her driveway, or watering her grass.

- Make a playdate with some of your younger neighbors and siblings. Set up story time in a backyard with blankets and snacks such as cookies and juice boxes. Read one of your childhood favorites, and then play a few fun games, such as Duck, Duck, Goose and Tag.

Performing Posse

If you chose **more c's,** you're an active group of girls who love to work hard. Try the following ideas, all of which will put a new spin on your sportiness:

- As a group, create a choreographed routine using hula hoops, jump ropes, or even basketballs. Try ripples (one person starts and then the next person repeats the action, and so on), group tricks, and adding music. Perform your routine for your family or friends.

- Create a secret handshake that's an elaborate routine of claps, shakes, spins, or other movements.

- Try a new sport! Gather some equipment and hit the nearest park to try a few drills, such as dribbling a basketball or soccer ball, hitting underhand softball pitches with a bat, shooting free throws, or kicking soccer balls into a goal. Any of your friends who have experience can help coach the other girls.

Babysitting Blues

The kids you're watching are getting restless, and you're stumped. Take this quiz to make your babysitting job a bit easier.

1. What do the kids enjoy?
a. coloring
b. playing outside
c. reading

2. The kids want to be _____ when they grow up.
a. actors
b. professional athletes
c. world travelers

3. The kids always get excited when I say,
a. "Let's watch a movie!"
b. "Let's draw with chalk outside!"
c. "Let's pretend!"

4. On their shelves, you see
a. activity books.
b. board games.
c. coloring books.

5. The stories they like best are about
a. being famous.
b. playing games.
c. made-up places.

6. After their parents leave, the kids are always
a. outgoing.
b. energetic.
c. shy.

7. The kids' favorite way to pass the time is
a. dancing and singing.
b. running and jumping.
c. story time and coloring.

8. The kids would love it if I
a. taught them a song.
b. played catch in the yard.
c. performed a magic trick for them.

9. The kids' toys are mostly
a. dress-up costumes.
b. sports equipment.
c. stuffed animals.

Answers

Starring You

If you chose **more a's,** the kids you watch will love to use their creativity to make their own show. After all, there's nothing more fun than being a star! Re-create a popular book or movie. Tell them that you're the director and you're looking for talented actors. The kids can design their own costumes and help you write a script. Perform the show for the parents when they get home.

Awesome Obstacles

If you chose **more b's,** the kids you watch are energetic and love to play outside. Turn the backyard or driveway into an obstacle course. Use chalk, balls, jump ropes, and sports equipment to create stations. Set requirements, such as "5 jumping jacks, 1 round of hopscotch, 2 laps around the tree, 3 jumps with the jump rope, and then shoot a basketball into the net!" Time the kids, and then ask them to set up an obstacle course for you. When the parents get home, they might even give the course a try!

Hide-and-Seek

If you chose **more c's,** the kids you watch may be a little shy. A scavenger hunt is a perfect way to help them warm up to you. Ask the kids to gather a few of their stuffed animals. While they watch TV for a few minutes, hide the stuffed animals around the house (not too high or in spots that are too hard to find). If the kids are really young, give them clues by saying "hot" if they're close and "cold" if they're far away. If the kids are older, you can write down rhyming clues that lead them to the correct room. Time them, and give them a little prize when they're done.

Keep the kids smiling with these fun activities until their parents arrive:

• Bring a board game that the kids don't have. Teach them how to play, and ask them to teach you how to play a game they like.

• Bring one of their children's books to life. Help the kids act it out and create new stories with the characters.

• Set up a doodle school. Teach the kids how to draw a fun doodle of yours.

• Write up a "Kid Questionnaire" and interview the kids about their likes and dislikes so that you can get to know them better. Then let them quiz you.

• Let the kids choose new names, and call them by their chosen names for the rest of the day. Be sure to give yourself a new name, too!

• Check out activity books from the library to share with the kids. Look for books with seek-and-find puzzles, jokes, and riddles.

• Help the kids write personal poems. Think of words that rhyme with their names and things they love to do.

Vacation Vocation

You're with your family but you're not at home. Time for some faraway family fun!

1. On this vacation, we're going to
   a. have a lot of free time.
   b. visit a huge amusement park.
   c. see a lot of sights in a fun city.

2. On family vacations, we usually
   a. relax a lot.
   b. have a full schedule of activities to fill the day.
   c. do something adventurous.

3. My family is mostly
   a. talkative.
   b. creative.
   c. energetic.

4. Everyone in my family likes to
   a. play games.
   b. take photos.
   c. read a lot.

5. As a family, we like to
   a. watch movies together.
   b. go camping together.
   c. ride bikes together.

6. When it comes to the past, I love
   a. telling stories.
   b. looking through photo albums.
   c. making new memories.

7. We never travel without a
   a. deck of cards.
   b. camera.
   c. guide book or brochure.

51

Answers

Conversation Starters

If you picked **more a's,** your family enjoys kicking back and spending quality time together. Bring a pack of blank note cards on your trip. Divide the cards up among your family members, and ask them all to write one conversation starter—something everyone in the family can respond to—on each card. For example:

- What's your earliest memory?
- What is/was your favorite subject in school?
- If you could be anything, what would it be?
- What nickname do your friends call you?
- What's your favorite piece of clothing?
- Tell an embarrassing story.

Family members take turns drawing a conversation starter, reading it aloud, and responding. They then pass the card to the next person so everyone has a chance to share.

Memory Keeper

If you picked **more b's,** your family likes to fill every minute of every vacation day with fun, fun, fun! Take a little bit of time each night to document the highlights of the day in a travel scrapbook or on a family blog. During the day, be sure to capture fun photos or cool trinkets from your travels. Ask everyone in your family to share their highlights from the day, and write those down (or type them up). When you finally make it back home, you can reminisce by rereading your vacation experiences.

Traveling Tour Guide

If you picked **more c's,** your family is a bunch of true-blue explorers! Ask each member of the family to research a landmark that he or she would like to visit. When you make it there, that family member has to teach everyone else all about it. At the end of the trip, vote on who was the best tour guide—who had the most interesting stories, or the best tour guide voice, and who chose the coolest landmark. You can also take turns reading from a guidebook as you travel. Where do you want to go next?

Study Support

If studying is giving you the yawns, then this quiz is for you! Find out which trick will help make memorizing vocab words or times tables the most fun!

1. At school, I like it when my teacher
   a. turns the lesson into a game.
   b. lets us work on homework alone.
   c. reads aloud in class.

2. I'm best at remembering
   a. general ideas.
   b. specific names and dates.
   c. pictures and stories.

3. For fun, I like to
   a. watch a movie.
   b. play a trivia game.
   c. read a book.

4. I can tell you
   a. that I have a project due sometime next week.
   b. the middle names and birthdays of everyone in my family.
   c. exactly what I wore on the first day of school last year.

5. I never remember my sneakers unless I
- **a.** ask my mom to remind me.
- **b.** write myself a note.
- **c.** set them right next to my backpack.

6. I stay organized by
- **a.** getting help from my family.
- **b.** writing in a daily planner.
- **c.** hanging a giant calendar over my desk.

7. When I watch a movie, I remember
- **a.** the story line and a good quote.
- **b.** every character's name and age.
- **c.** what the opening scene looked like.

Test Friday

Answers

Study Show

If you answered **more a's,** ask family members to quiz you by reading questions out loud. Pretend you're buzzing in on a game show. If you get stuck, ask them to help you come up with memory tricks. Write the tricks down and study them so that you'll nail the question the next time around.

Remember
- Bake Sale today
- Report due Tues.
- Student assembly Friday

Flash Bash

If you answered **more b's,** you have a great memory! Make flash cards by writing a question on the front of a blank note card and the answer on the back. Shuffle the cards and begin to quiz yourself. When you answer a card correctly, set it to the side. Keep repeating the deck until you've answered all the questions correctly and set all cards to the side. Now gather the cards back up and try again. Time yourself to see how long it takes to answer them all correctly.

A+

Pass the Class

If you answered **more c's,** reteaching the topic may help jog your memory. Set up a classroom in your bedroom with your stuffed animals. Now pretend that you are the teacher and your stuffed animals are a new class of students. Teach them all about your test topics. Explain out loud everything they need to know, and use a small wipe-off board to illustrate the ideas. Helping others learn will help you understand!

Don't forget Sneakers!

game
Mon.

A happy surprise is right around the corner

Your enthusiasm for life will take you far.

Here are a few more ways to make studying a little less work and a little more fun:

• Make up a song, rhyme, or poem to help you remember those pesky facts you're struggling with.

• Take a break! If you feel stressed or sleepy, take 5 minutes to get a healthy snack or drink, or do 5 jumping jacks. A break can help you focus later.

• Imagine the topic as a movie or TV show. Who are the main characters? What's the story?

• Turn the facts into a visual display to help you remember them—try a scrapbook, a timeline, or a comic strip.

• Create a trivia game. Invite a classmate over to play, and you'll both get some studying done.

• Write important facts on sticky notes and stick them to a wall. When you memorize one, take it down.

• Instead of reading to yourself, read out loud—with a funny accent!

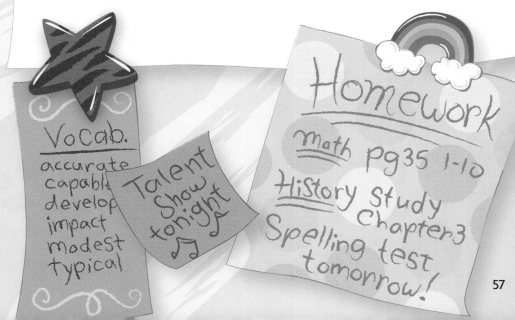

Vocab.
accurate
capable
develop
impact
modest
typical

Talent
Show
tonight ♪

Homework
math pg35 1-10
History study
chapter 3
Spelling test
tomorrow!

Mom & Me Morning

You need some "Mom and me" time. Plan a special weekend morning to spend together, and use this quiz to find out what the two of you should do.

1. Your mom and you both like
   a. watching movies.
   b. playing sports.
   c. decorating cupcakes.

2. You'd love to
   a. know what your mom was like when she was younger.
   b. know how to do something your mom is good at doing.
   c. try something new with your mom.

3. When it comes to helping your mom, you do so by
   a. entertaining your siblings.
   b. putting away your sports equipment after practice.
   c. cleaning up after dinner.

4. Your mom loves to talk to you about
   a. what you learned at school.
   b. your hobbies.
   c. what treats you want for this weekend's sleepover.

5. You think your mom's _____ is so cool.
   a. childhood scrapbook
   b. pair of old ballet shoes
   c. all-time best recipe

6. Recently, your mom helped you
   a. get through a problem you had with a friend.
   b. French-braid your hair before a big soccer game.
   c. come up with a cool idea for a school project.

7. Like you, your mom
   a. reads a lot.
   b. plays an instrument.
   c. loves to paint.

Answers

Hooked on Books

If you chose **more a's,** start a Mom-and-me book club. Ask your mom to create a list of her favorite books from when she was about your age. Add your current favorites, and choose a book to start with. Spend your next Mom-and-me morning discussing the book. Answer questions such as these:

- What part did you like best?
- Did you like the ending?
- How would you have changed the story?
- Which character is most like you?

New for the Two of You

If you chose **more b's,** try something new with your mom. Decide on an activity you're both interested in. Maybe it's a long ride down a bike path or a trip to a new bakery downtown. Having a little adventure with your mom will give you both a great memory and a fun story to share with your family. If you love it, you can start a monthly tradition.

Kitchen Session

If you chose **more c's,** open a Mom-and-me restaurant in your own kitchen. Plan an exciting breakfast that your family will love, and then help your mom make it. Start by choosing a theme. It could be a country, a holiday, fancy foods, or foods that start with the letter P. Write down a list of your ingredients, and make a trip to the grocery store if needed. If your meal is a success, write the information on a handmade recipe card—or even start your own Mom-and-me cookbook.

Pleasant Trails

Dad & Daughter Day

Does Dad have some time to spare? What should the two of you do? Answer these questions to figure out an awesome activity that you and your dad will love.

1. Just like you, your dad is
   a. creative.
   b. laid-back.
   c. athletic.

2. You'd love to
   a. work on a project with your dad.
   b. try something new with your dad.
   c. have a friendly competition with your dad.

3. Your dad and you both like
   a. solving problems.
   b. the outdoors.
   c. playing games.

4. When it comes to your dad, you can always find him
   a. in his workshop.
   b. doing yard work.
   c. on the computer.

5. You and your dad love to watch _____ on TV.
   a. cooking shows
   b. travel shows
   c. sporting events

6. You think your dad's _____ is so cool.
   a. tool set
   b. camping tent
   c. bike

7. You and your dad both play
   a. musical instruments.
   b. catch in the backyard.
   c. competitive sports.

8. When your family is at the beach, you and your dad
   a. like to take lots of pictures.
   b. rent a kayak or wakeboards.
   c. race to see who can build the biggest sand castle.

9. When it comes to homework, your dad
   a. helps you create a cool science project.
   b. calms you down when you're stressed out.
   c. quizzes you before a big test.

Answers

Happy Hobby

If you picked **more a's,** you both love to work with your hands. Why not start a project together? Take a trip to the craft store or hobby shop. Try putting together a huge puzzle, building a dollhouse from scratch, or assembling a model. It's a project that might turn into a dad-daughter hobby. When you're done, you'll both be proud of the work you accomplished together!

Outdoor Adventure

If you picked **more b's,** you both love the outdoors. Today's the perfect day to get outside and enjoy the day together. Is your dad a hiker, biker, fisherman, cross-country skier, or golfer? Ask him to show you the ropes. See if you can rent equipment, and then start your adventure together. You wont be perfect at first, but you can learn a lot from your dad. Soon you might have a new activity that both you and your dad love!

Game Day

If you picked **more c's,** you and your dad are both athletic. Take that energy and stage a friendly competition—a video-game competition. Play games at home or visit the arcade. Play 3 rounds of each game to give each other a fair shot at mastering some new skills. Make sure to share tips and tricks! Ask the rest of your family to join in afterward for some just-for-fun playing time.

**Try some of these activities for
fun with the whole family:**

• Pick one night of the week to make dinner
together and watch a movie or TV show you all love.

• Try a new sport. Create a family bowling
league or take tennis lessons together.

• Do two or more of you play an instrument?
Start a family band. Learn a song that
you can perform together.

• Include the family pet in your next outing.
Make him or her a part of a trip to the park,
family movie night in the living room, or a
barbecue in the backyard.

• Ask your parents to teach you a board game
or card game they liked to play when
they were kids.

• Compare school photos of yourself
and your parents at the same ages.
Decorate a frame and display photos side by side.

• Have a movie night—starring you and your family!
Instead of letting old family movies gather dust, enjoy
funny footage from vacations and family events.

Best-Friend Blast

You love spending time with your BFF, but you two are looking for something extra fun today. Take this quiz together.

1. We love to
   a. read.
   b. make crafts.
   c. talk.

2. Today we want to try something
   a. new.
   b. creative.
   c. BIG.

3. People think we're sisters because we
   a. finish each other's sentences.
   b. share everything.
   c. think the same thoughts.

4. Someday, we'd love to _____ together.
   a. write a book
   b. design a line of clothing
   c. start a company

5. For birthday presents, we usually give each other
   a. handmade gifts.
   b. something cool we've been eyeing for months.
   c. a trip to the movie theater or bowling alley.

6. We're best friends because
   a. we've known each other forever.
   b. we make each other laugh.
   c. we have the same interests.

7. To cheer each other up, we
   a. send each other nice e-mails.
   b. bring each other a treat to eat.
   c. do something fun together, such as ride bikes.

Answers

Pal Tale

If you chose **more a's,** write the story of your friendship. But there's a catch—you have to take turns writing. Pass a piece of lined paper back and forth. Take turns, each of you writing one sentence at a time about your friendship. One of you might remember something that the other forgot, or you might find yourself writing about all your friend's best qualities. When you're done, you'll put smiles on each other's faces and have a special story to share with others.

Here are some sentences to get you started:

- It all started the day we met.
- There are many reasons why we're friends.
- It was our most fun day together.
- Some people think we're sisters.
- Friends are always there for each other.
- We're like two peas in a pod.
- You might say that we can read each other's minds.

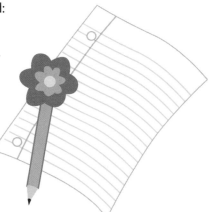

Design Duo

If you chose **more b's,** you're a crafty pair. You two have very similar tastes, so you probably know exactly what kind of bracelet your friend would like to wear. Spend the afternoon making super-special handmade friendship bracelets—but then swap with each other! Take three long lengths of ribbon and braid them. Do so by asking your friend to hold the ends for you while you braid. String a charm onto one ribbon at the center, and then continue braiding. Now switch places and make another. Give the bracelets to each other when you're done.

Buddy Business

If you chose **more c's,** you and your friend work well together. Why not start a business? Spend today brainstorming what your business could be. Is it a simple lemonade stand? A babysitting service? Birthday-party planning? Think of what you're good at, the needs of your neighborhood, and the supplies you already have. Together you can have fun and earn a little bit of money.

Write Now

Need to write something for school but stuck in a writing rut? Find the perfect story starter for you.

1. On a Saturday, you can find me
   a. painting in a community art class.
   b. cheering at a basketball game.
   c. reading at the library.

2. One word that describes me is
   a. creative.
   b. outgoing.
   c. shy.

3. When the day is dull, I
   a. daydream.
   b. call a friend.
   c. watch TV or a movie.

4. People always tell me I'm
   a. good at making things.
   b. athletic.
   c. quiet.

5. If my life were a sport, it would be
   a. gymnastics.
   b. basketball.
   c. swimming.

6. When I doodle, I draw
  a. little animals and creatures.
  b. my name.
  c. shapes like stars and circles.

7. If I wanted to do a relaxing activity, I would
  a. read a magazine.
  b. play a video game.
  c. listen to music.

8. My dream birthday party would be going with friends
  a. to a pottery-making class.
  b. to play laser tag.
  c. on a trip to the spa.

9. If I were in a school play, I would be
  a. a costume designer.
  b. the star.
  c. a part of the backstage crew.

Answers

Picture This

If you answered **more a's,** find inspiration in an image. Look to family photos, an art-class drawing, or a book cover. Create a story based on that image. Maybe a picture of a lake sparks your imagination to write a camp story. Or a girl standing alone on the cover of a novel inspires you to write a story about friendship. Keep flipping through books, magazines, and pictures until something catches your eye.

Phrase Craze

If you answered **more b's,** you need something a bit more exciting to get you in the mood to write. On one piece of paper, write down a bunch of places, such as "Florida" or "a middle school." On a second piece, write down a bunch of characters, such as "a teacher" or "a cute puppy." On a third piece, write down different activities, such as "ice-skating" or "conducting a science experiment."

Cut out the phrases, fold them up, and place them in three different bowls—one for each category. Choose strips from each bowl until you find a combination that inspires you. Now get writing!

Fickle Fiction

If you answered **more c's,** you are calmer and quieter than your friends. But what if your story isn't? Write a story about people or things that are the complete opposite of you—where they live, what they like, and how they act. Maybe your story is about a singer from Georgia who is really funny and likes to play soccer. Write about what you **don't** know—it will jump-start your imagination!

Outdoor Action

The sun is shining and you want to spend the day breathing in the fresh air. What should you do today?

1. When I wake up to a beautiful day, I want to
   a. call up all my friends and ask them to come over.
   b. spend all day outside.
   c. relax on my own.

2. I live near mostly
   a. other kids.
   b. shops and restaurants.
   c. parks.

3. I have a lot of
   a. sports equipment.
   b. art supplies.
   c. snack recipes.

4. I'm really good at
   a. directing a group of friends.
   b. making things with my hands.
   c. organizing a party.

5. I have most fun when I spend time with
   a. a big group of friends.
   b. my best friend.
   c. a few close friends.

6. I use my _____ the most.
   a. sneakers
   b. calculator
   c. apron

7. My only pet peeve about summer is that
   a. my friends are sometimes gone on vacation.
   b. the days aren't long enough!
   c. there are too many mosquitoes and bugs. Yuck!

Answers

Relay-Race Rally

If you chose **more a's,** call up your friends and neighbors for some relay fun! Ask an adult to act as the referee—to say "Go!" and make sure that every-one is following the rules. These games will be most fun if there are at least 3 players on each team. Play these games in a big yard with a chair set about 10 paces in front of each team.

Here are some ideas to get you started:

• Each player on the team holds a balloon. On "Go," the first player walks quickly to the chair and pops the balloon by sitting on it. Then the player walks back and tags someone to go next.

• The first player on the team holds a spoon and a plastic egg. Each player must take turns walking forward, around the chair, and back without dropping the egg. Then that player passes the spoon to the next player.

• Each player on the team must walk backward carefully up to and around the chair and back. Tag the next player until all players have had a turn.

Sunny-Day Scoop Shop

If you chose **more b's,** take advantage of the good weather and set up an "ice cream shop" with a twist—it's melt-free! Invite a friend to help scoop pudding or yogurt into cones and then top with sprinkles for a treat that looks like ice cream but doesn't need to be frozen. Ask a parent to make a cone holder by cutting 2 rows of X's into the front of a cereal box. When your customers order, offer different toppings, such as mini chocolate chips, caramel sauce, and, of course, a cherry on top!

Pack a Picnic

If you chose **more c's,** all you need is a blanket, a tote bag, and some finger food to pack a perfect picnic for your family or friends. Include foods like these:

• sandwiches such as peanut butter and jelly or ham and Swiss cheese
• bananas, apples, or grapes
• granola bars, string cheese, potato chips, or any other individually packaged snacks
• water bottles or juice boxes
• napkins and plates

Pack your supplies in a tote bag, and roll up a blanket and tie it with a ribbon so that it's easy to carry. Set up your picnic in your own backyard, at a park, or at the beach. Take plenty of time to share the food and fun. After all, it's a beautiful day!

The Big List

Tried everything in this book but still searching for more fun? Pick a task from this list and banish the boredom blues!

- Write a song about your pet.
- Make up a dance and teach it to your friends or siblings.
- Teach yourself how to count to ten in another language.
- Write a letter to a faraway cousin or friend.
- Make a handmade gift for your grandpa or grandma.
- Design your dream house—inside and out.
- Write a story about who you think you'll be when you grow up.
- Make up a secret code and write a letter in code to your friend.
- Write a new ending to a popular book or movie.
- Make up new abbreviations like "gr8" for "great" or "ttyl" for "talk to you later."
- Make up new rules to your favorite game.
- Memorize a scene from a movie and act it out with friends.
- Plan a dream vacation to a faraway place.
- Reread a book series you love from start to finish.
- Try a hairstyle that you've never tried before.
- Ask a parent if you can help with chores around the house.
- Watch a familiar movie with the sound off and act out the lines with friends.
- Organize pictures of your friends and family and display them in your room.
- Write new lyrics to a current hit song.
- Offer to help a sibling or friend clean her room.
- Find an old board game that you haven't played in a while.
- Draw a self-portrait using only bright colors.
- Create a comic starring an animal as a superhero.
- Draw a map of your neighborhood as if it's a treasure map.

What was your favorite quiz and activity? Tell us!

Mail to:

Bored No More Editor

American Girl

8400 Fairway Place

Middleton, WI 53562

(All comments and suggestions received by American Girl
may be used without compensation or acknowledgment.
Sorry—photos can't be returned.)

Here are some other American Girl books you might like.

Each sold separately. Find more books online at americangirl.com.